PRAISE FOR

Sunset

"Using the haiku form, sparse and powerful, Jane paints pictures resonating with meaning—beautiful, candid, and honest."

—Steve Hammond, founding head, St. Patrick Catholic School, Norfolk, VA; poet, musician,

"Loving tributes to nature, family, friends, and faith, all delivered with self-deprecation and maternal care. Though life has given her, in her own words, 'the easier race,' Jane has run as fast as her pen and heart could take her to arrive at this impressive *Sunset* collection of liberation poems."

—Page Laws, dean emerita, Nusbaum Honors College at Norfolk State University; theater and opera critic for *The Virginian Pilot*

"Jane has accomplished what many have only contemplated: bringing a book idea to publication. In so doing, she reminds us that every day is a new opportunity to pursue our creative goals."

—John S. Dixon, executive director, Academy of Music, Norfolk, VA; organist and composer

Sunset

by Jane Batten

© Copyright 2025 Jane Batten
ISBN 979-8-88824-803-4

All rights reserved. No part of this publication may be reproduced, stored in a retrieval system, or transmitted in any form or by any means—electronic, mechanical, photocopy, recording, or any other—except for brief quotations in printed reviews, without the prior written permission of the author.

This is a work of fiction. All the characters in this book are fictitious, and any resemblance to actual persons, living or dead, is purely coincidental. The names, incidents, dialogue, and opinions expressed are products of the author's imagination and are not to be construed as real.

Published by

3705 Shore Drive
Virginia Beach, VA 23455
800-435-4811
www.koehlerbooks.com

SUNSET

Poems by

JANE BATTEN

VIRGINIA BEACH
CAPE CHARLES

For Mary Oliver
1935–2019

Poems are music.
Oh, Mary, what would I do
Without your sweet songs?

CONTENTS

Part 1: Nature 3

Part 2: Places 21

Part 3: Family and Friends 33

Part 4: Church 47

Part 5: Love 57

Part 6: Triples 67

Epilogue 73

THOUGHTS ON SUNSETS

After a hot summer's day,
The Sun is surely tired
From lighting the world,
Needing a cooling dip in the Bay.

Yet, even in a dreary spell,
She takes the time to paint the clouds
Her pink and gold farewell.

Brother Moon, the lazy one,
Just comes and goes,
Except on the night he's full of himself.

Not Sister Sun.
Every evening, seen or not,
She works at her easel in the sky.

PART 1

Nature

CONSERVATION

I've left it too late
To tell a tale worth reading.
Another tree saved.

SNOW

The first snowflakes come
Riding in on salty air,
Decorating dunes.

NOR'EASTER

The storm has not passed.
White breakers still scour wet sand
For hidden treasures.

CONTAINER SHIP

Carrying truckloads,
Black behemoth of the sea,
Filling my window.

SUNDAY DINNER

Daisies in a jug.
Country cousins come to call
Sunday after church.

BEACH

Morning on the beach,
Sun exploding from the sea,
Rollers singing bass.

BROOK

Does the icy brook
Sing and laugh out loud seeing
Children's wading toes?

LUCK

Pale four-leaf clover;
Luck to one who spies it there
Hiding in the turf.

SAND

Precious grains of sand,
Building grassy dunes that hold
An ocean at bay.

FALL

First meal of autumn;
Chew the cooling northern winds,
Sip the winey air.

BOUQUET

Buttercup bouquet.
Picked by grubby hands to take
Wilting home to Mom.

OCEAN

The winter ocean,
Really angry, really loud.
Roaring at the dunes.

PART 2

Places

WELLINGTON

Family graveyard;
Shore names you would recognize,
But where are the slaves?

HARBOUR ISLAND

Little island town,
Colonial past still found.
Light blue eyes, skin brown.

CHAUTAUQUA

Eden by a lake
Calls to me when the ice melts
And the docks are in.

DORNOCH

Linked gems down a coast,
Eighteen reasons to return.
Gorse a golden blaze.

COBB ISLAND STATION

Brave men launched their boats
And rowed to rescue wrecked ships
Pounding on a shoal.

UTAH

Dinosaur footprints,
Red arches framing vistas
Of a West that was.

HOLLINS

Tinker standing guard
Over a beloved place
Where young women bloom.

OAKENCROFT

Green farm on green hills;
Cattle, sheep, and vines, all raised
To husband God's gifts.

PORCH TIME

The best time of day,
When we share what matters most
On a seaside porch.

PART 3

Family and Friends

Photo by Dorothy Batten

GRANDOG

Luli, nine breeds strong,
A golden-coated huntress,
At prey on the dunes.

SUNDAYS

You riding shotgun;
Happy Sundays together
On our way to church.

THE FIVE

Gallant one-eyed five;
Seeing more than others who
Just make do with two.

OLD FRIENDS

Old souls, John and Jane.
Pisces both, a water sign.
Friendship oceans deep.

DADS

I had two fathers,
Both a blessing, both a gift
To open each day.

NEAL

I have a brother,
One my mother cannot claim.
Bonds stronger than blood.

THE BOY

Thirty-seven times
They moved somewhere, but nowhere
The boy could call home.

PUFF

Puff works his magic
On a crowd of friends who sense
His endless wonder.

DANCING QUEEN

Feet moving swiftly,
Twirling around, stepping out
To a Polka beat.

FLIGHT

A wise friend told me
The runway's getting shorter.
Is it time to land?

SUFFRAGETTES

Eliza, marching
For the vote, shouting for their
Demands to be heard.

PART 4

Church

Photo by Dorothy Batten

ICELAND—2023

Waiting for her flock,
Lonely chapel on a hill,
Faith the strongest chain.

CHURCH

Our Noah's stone ark,
Full of hungry worshipers,
Waiting to be fed.

THE WAR

I am not a prize.
Why have faith and reason fought
Such a long battle?

HOPE

In this darkened world,
Does there glow a bright sadness
That we can call hope?

JOHN 21

Feed my flock, He said.
Fill them with the Holy Stew,
The meat of Good News.

REASON

Distant door marked "Faith,"
Open to one who leaps, but
Reason tugs the reins.

ALTAR-CATION

An altar-cation.
Hearts ascend as Christ descends
Scaffolding and cross.

Contribution from D. R. B.
Christ & St. Luke's Episcopal Church, Norfolk, Virginia

Photo by Kevin Kwan

PART 5

Love

Photo by Megan Varner

ANOTHER STAR

Long before we met,
I had loved you forever
On another star.

TOO LATE

Love me now, he pled.
It's not soon enough, she said.
The leaves are falling.

NO REGRETS

Let's dance the last dance
Like we would have long ago:
Never looking back.

NEW FRIEND

Just begin as friends.
Go slow, let it grow, you'll know
When it turns to love.

LAKE

Standing by a lake.
Only then did I feel full,
Sated by your words.

LARKS

Don't let love be sad.
It should sing like larks and soar
Rising to the sun.

PART 6
Triples

RIVER 1943

In my brown tweed coat
And leggings, pulling my sled.
Sliding on the ice.

Lafayette frozen
Solid, to the other shore.
Safe to walk upon.

While in the summer
Mother rows across to work
In the hospital.

THE GIFT

The winds are too warm.
Waters often flood my road.
How long have we here?

I promised his gold,
When they ought to have had his
Hands, hard on the helm.

No comparisons.
You're all the other things I
Needed him to be.

LOVE x THREE

Down the long church aisle
She walks into her future;
Prince Charming awaits.

Yellowed photographs,
Sudden stabs of memory.
Longing thought long past.

Unlike a first love,
Late in life two souls building
A tie that will last.

EPILOGUE

FAREWELL

I'm like an athlete,
Training for the big event.
Practicing goodbye.

THE END

Soft from the cedars,
I heard the owl call my name.
The last reveille.

TO JOE

Where are you now?
Floating above the ether,
Young again and spry.
Did you see the light
And follow it to that new place?
Were you surprised
There really is a heaven?

In Memory of The Reverend Joseph N. Green, Jr.
1926–2023

ELECTION

Votes tell the story
Of the great divide.
Too many fall beside
The road to the big dream
Or never begin the walk.

Too many steps
To climb out of the crib
And onto the school bus.
Passage to a door of promise,
A chance to grow into yourself.

Too few born incumbents,
Given the easier race.

(Written shortly after November 5, 2024)

www.ingramcontent.com/pod-product-compliance
Lightning Source LLC
LaVergne TN
LVHW091545070526
838199LV00002B/218